Walk with Me Lord!

Thirty Day Journey to be Transformed

Zolisha L. Ware

Copyright © 2019 by Zolisha L. Ware

All rights reserved. No part of this publication may be reproduced by any means, graphics, electronic, or mechanical, including photocopying, recording, taping, or by any information storage retrieval system without the written permission of the publisher except in the case of brief quotations embodied in critical articles and reviews.

Zolisha L. Ware/Rejoice Essential Publishing
PO BOX 512
Effingham, SC 29541

www.republishing.org

Unless otherwise indicated, scripture is taken from the King James Version.

Scripture quotations marked (ESV) are taken from The Holy Bible, English Standard Version® (ESV®) Copyright © 2001 by Crossway, a publishing ministry of Good News Publishers. All rights reserved.

Scripture quotations marked (NIV) are taken from the Holy Bible, New International Version®, NIV®. Copyright © 1973, 1978, 1984, 2011 by Biblica, Inc.™ Used by permission of Zondervan. All rights reserved worldwide. www.zondervan.com The "NIV" and "New International Version" are trademarks registered in the United States Patent and Trademark Office by Biblica, Inc.™

Scripture quotations marked (NLT) are taken from the Holy Bible, New Living Translation, copyright ©1996, 2004, 2015 by Tyndale House Foundation. Used by permission of Tyndale House Publishers, a Division of Tyndale House Ministries, Carol Stream, Illinois 60188. All rights reserved.

"Scripture quotations taken from the New American Standard Bible® (NASB), Copyright © 1960, 1962, 1963, 1968, 1971, 1972, 1973, 1975, 1977, 1995 by The Lockman Foundation Used by permission. www.Lockman.org"

Walk with Me Lord!/ Zolisha L. Ware

ISBN-13: 978-1-952312-12-0

Library of Congress Control Number: 2020906668

Dedication

To my Lord and Savior, who delivered me out of the hands of the enemy. He healed and restored me for His namesake. Now, I may be of some use for the kingdom. In Him, I live and have my being. I am eternally grateful for my second chance to complete all that God called me to do. For His love covered and kept me until I was able to cover another.

This book was given unto me directly from the Holy Spirit. He was the first to arrest me with the Love of God and to correct me with that same love. He is teaching me to live a Kingdom centered life and allowing me to be transformed by the renewal of my mind. May that love transfer into every life that reads this book. It has created a renewed mind that has the desire to walk with the Lord.

Table of Contents

ACKNOWLEDGMENTS..................................xii

PREFACE...xiv

INTRODUCTION..1

DAY 1:   Spoken Words............................7

DAY 2:   Word Curses............................16

DAY 3:   Guard Our Tongues....................25

DAY 4:   Word Battle................................34

DAY 5:   Weekly Review..........................43

DAY 6:   Deceitful Tongue......................50

DAY 7:   Thoughtful Words....................59

DAY 8:   Life-Giving Words....................68

DAY 9:   Satisfying Words........................77

DAY 10:	Weekly Review..............................87
DAY 11:	Harmful Words............................94
DAY 12:	Mediator Words.........................103
DAY 13:	Words Empower........................112
DAY 14:	Idle Words..................................122
DAY 15:	Weekly Review..........................131
DAY 16:	Righteousness Words...............138
DAY 17:	Words of Wisdom......................147
DAY 18:	Prayer Life Build Right Words...............................156
DAY 19:	Quick and Power Words............166
DAY 20:	Weekly Review..........................176
DAY 21:	Pure Word.................................183

DAY 22:	Words that Stand Forever..........................192
DAY 23:	Fire & Hammer Words..............201
DAY 24:	Born Again Words.....................210
DAY 25:	Weekly Review...........................219
DAY 26:	Heavenly Words........................226
DAY 27:	Sweet Words..............................236
DAY 28:	Hearing Words..........................245
DAY 29:	Seed Producing Words..254
DAY 30:	Weekly Reflection....................263

CLOSING NOTES...270

ABOUT THE AUTHOR..................................285

Acknowledgments

I acknowledge my Lord and Savior, who healed my mouth from being defiled that I might help others. Timothy 3:16 says, "All scripture given by inspiration of God and is profitable for doctrine, for reproof, for correction, for instruction in righteousness."

Secondly, I want to give acknowledgment to my husband, whom I love very much. He always encourages me to write and teach according to my portion. He continually reminds me to be who God has called me. His love and support helps me to stay focused and fulfill the call before me.

Next, I would like to shout out my children, who helped me be a better mom, and child of God by holding me accountable in my infant stage of being a Christian. I love you and may the fruit of my life bring everlasting seed to yours.

Lastly, I want to give a special shout out to my present and future supporters.

Preface

This devotion "Walk with Me" developed from a series on my Facebook page for about three years. After many years of allowing the Lord to walk with me, I began to disclose lessons learned from the Holy Spirit to help others understand there is help in our daily walk with Christ. My first lessons were on the words I used and how they affected me. Many talk without really understanding the meanings of words or the interpretation of them. Although some of this is due to cultural disparities, other times are just a lack of understanding as a whole. In most school systems depending on the location of the school, many institutions don't take the time to help those who lack comprehension skills to gain them. Then those individuals get into the body of Christ, and they struggle with understanding God's Word because those skills have never developed. I was one who struggled with some reading skills. Due to an eye injury at eight years old, and ever since that injury, words on the pages sometimes move around. I had to focus on those words to stabilize. However, even in that, my God has granted me mercy and grace to study the Bible and has helped me to interpret them using the Holy Ghost. I give this example only to say that every issue you have no matter what it is, the Lord can help you overcome that issue that you may be of some use for His kingdom. However, it's our responsibility and duty to study to show ourselves approved not for judgment but a refinement to be ushered out to the highways and bye-ways to minister to all those within the world.

This devotional journal is to help you understand the importance of the Word of God and how you speak those words over your life. How many times do we take the terms we use for granted? Proverbs 18:21 reads, "Death and life are in the power of the tongue: and they that love it shall eat the fruit thereof." When you speak, a decision made willingly or unwillingly can produce or destroy the fruit of your life. We have to take more time to pay attention to our words so that we don't curse ourselves, which would cause more significant destruction than what others cause to us. If we learned how to speak affirmations and proclamations unto ourselves, we can heal our lives, help others improve, and share our tools. This devotional journal is just that—my secret weapon to freedom from the statistics I put myself in within my unlearned state. With every word, I learned to build my self-confidence, overcome difficulty and decree what God already said He promised. Putting God's Word into action caused me to see a change in my life and those around me. So, I share these tips with you that you will be all that God called you to be.

Introduction

WORDS HAVE POWER

Have you ever heard someone say that you're beautiful or handsome? Have you ever told yourself you are beautiful or handsome? How did that make you feel? Did you smile? Did your walk change? I can see you smiling ear to ear. Oh, how words are powerful! Oh, how important the right words are to the building of our lives. I was set free by four words said to me by the Holy Spirit, "Do you love me?" Those words shifted my life and brought me out of twenty-six years of oppression from the enemy. Words can free us or cause us to be bound. Thus, as the body of believers, we must guard our words because one day we all will give an account for every spoken word given in this life.

DEFINITION:
Word

Noun - A single distinct meaningful element of speech or writing, used with others (or sometimes alone) to form a sentence and typically shown with space on either side when written or printed.

Verb - Choose and use particular words to say or write (something).

Affirmation - the act of affirming or something affirmed: a positive assertion.[1]

Exhortation - language intended to incite and encourage.[2]

---

1. Webster, M. (2020, February 22). Affirmation. Retrieved from Merriam Webster: https://www.merriam-webster.com/dictionary/affirmation
2. 2020 Merriam-Webster, I. (2020, February 22). Exhortation. Retrieved from Merriam Webster: https://www.merriam-webster.com/dictionary/exhortation

Proclamation - the action of proclaiming: the state of being proclaimed or something proclaimed.[3]

Exclamation - Used to agree.

Your words have the power to build up or tear down. The four terms to change my life forever were given to me by the Holy Spirit, "Do you love me?" as I previously stated. At the time, I didn't know how to answer those words because I was so broken. I didn't have a clue about love. The dictionary says love is a strong affection for another arising out of kinship or personal ties of affection based on admiration, benevolence, or common interests or assurance of affection.[4] We know that God's Word says in John 3:16, "For God so loved the world, that he gave his only begotten Son, that whosoever believeth in him should not perish, but have everlasting life." Which tells us Jesus is love. God loves me so much He sent the Holy Spirit to ask me that question three times.

---

3. 2020 Merriam-Webster, I. (2020, February 22). Proclamation. Retrieved from Merriam Webster: https://www.merriam-webster.com/dictionary/proclamation
4. 2019 Merriam-Webster, I. (2019, May 28). Love. Retrieved from Merriam Webster: https://www.merriam-webster.com/dictionary/love

My answer to that question determined if I would continue to live or if I would bust hell wide open. Thus, this book is born out of that. The very first point of correction from God was my mouth. How could He use a mouth full of fifth and a mouth that destroyed herself every chance she got? Many of you today reading this book are in the shoes I was many years ago. You're looking for God to do something great in your life. However, your tongue is getting in the way. As quick as God blesses, then you destroy. After you study this book, I decree that the members of your tongue will be under subjection. I decree freedom in your speech, understanding, and thinking. I decree that your mouth is healed, and the fire of God will come and fill your mouth. That the fire of God will consume anything not like Him until your words are seasoned with grace, love, and compassion every time they are used. I speak all these things in Jesus' name Amen.

Within this devotional, you will gain insight into the power of God's Word for your life. You will learn how there is nothing in your life that God hasn't addressed in His world. We will discuss how words can become blessings or curses.

Quickening in you (the understanding that if you speak negatively) those things become curses that can destroy your life and those whom we have spoken them over. Many of our words spoken have been adopted in our culture as social norms; however, when we research the root of those words, we find them connected to demonic influences. These influences open the door to demons that come to destroy us before we ever reach the destiny ordained by God. However, God teaches us that in all our getting, get wisdom: and with all thy getting get understanding (Proverbs 4:7). We will not conform to this world but continue our journey FAITHFUL as we pass through this corrupt and unjust world.

INSTRUCTIONS

If you have read any of my books, you will notice I believe in learning. This book is no different. The Bible tells us to study to show ourselves approved. Which means to study to show ourselves worthy unto God for the use of service since we all should have a servant mentality. We will put this into action. Every day you will have meditation verses and words. My motto is practice makes permanent. Which simply put means: whatever you practice regularly will be what you do on an everyday basis. If you practice cheating, you will be good at cheating others. Thus, if you practice guarding your tongue only to speak life, your mouth will be a living foundation ready for use unto the Father. God cannot use a defiled boaster's tongue. That tongue will tear down everything it can. Therefore, let's take some time to use words to deliver, heal, and launch us to our next destination in life. The more you practice the Word and Scriptures, the stronger you will become.

SPOKEN WORDS

Proverbs 11:17
Your soul is nourished when you are kind, but you destroy yourself when you are cruel.

The word spoken is defined as delivered by word of mouth: ORAL.[5] Spoken words can be given directly from your mouth or the mouths of others. Depending on the nature of the terms <u>and who gives</u> them, they can carry significant

5. 2019 Merriam-Webster, I. (2019, May 24). Oral Retrieved from Merriam Webster Dictionary: https://www.merriam-webster.com/dictionary/oral

weight. Thus, we must guard our hearts not to take on words designed to destroy us. However, we must allow those words designed to correct, guide, and build to have perfect work in us that we may fulfill the very destiny for which we are created.

DEVOTION

Many of us want mercy; however, we don't want to extend forgiveness to others. Instead, we create self-sufficient requirements for the person, which will allow them to continue to operate within our lives. However, we're guarded. God gives us renewed mercy every day. So, why are we not allowing others to have that same grace? We are supposed to be the children of God and supposed to operate according to the example that was sent through Jesus. Psalms 112:4-9 states, "Unto the upright there ariseth light in the darkness." He is gracious and full of compassion, and righteous. Jesus showed compassion for all. No matter the status or offense, He was merciful. To have the right attributes of Christ, we must be merciful to all even when they are continuing to display offensive behavior. Remember some things God can instantly heal, and some things take time. Extending mercy to others allows them the grace to perfect their walk to become more Christ-like while building everlasting character in you.

I can remember I used to have a close relationship with a person who was a fornicator. She continually slept with married men. I had to confront her concerning her behavior when I did, she broke down and said she didn't understand why she continued the practice. We talked and cried about the issues she had, and I prayed with her. I thought the issue was resolved, but it wasn't long before I found out she was at it again. I became so angry because I thought she was over the problem. But really, what I was doing was super sainting her, which is when a person tries to fix something without really taking it to the Father.

No one can genuinely heal without our Lord and Savior. I had to put her on the altar and ask God to deliver her. Matthew 15:26 states deliverance is the children's bread. Since we know, bread is food, and we need food daily for nourishment. Deliverance can be viewed as a daily activity used to keep us healed and free. We think because we talk and cry, things are resolved with people. However, God had to come in and get to the root of the issue. He had to heal her heart and allow her to see her value. As people, we only know the problem, but God looks at the heart. We, as children of God, need to take more time examining hearts and less time focusing on the outward man. All life issues should examine through our Father in Heaven's eyes that we may resolve those issues, not continue cycles that can destroy us and keep us from meeting our destiny. Psalm 41:1 says, "Blessed is he that considered the poor: the LORD will deliver him in time of trouble." Remember, a person can be deficient in more things than money. They can be lacking in character. This is why you need to carry mercy around with you daily. Your attitude will never be changed as the results of other people's behaviors.

SELF-EVALUATION

Do you examine every word that comes out of your mouth?

How often do you extend mercy to others?

PRAYER

Dear Heavenly Father, I ask you to help me show mercy and grace to all who come before me. Please help me to guard my words that they may be filled with kindness. Lord, allow me to see the heart of man beyond what is shown before me. Lord, help me to be delivered from hurtful words spoken over me and those who denied me mercy in my shortcomings. And protect my ears of the words released to me. In Jesus' name. Amen.

REFLECTION:

_____

_____

_____

_____

_____

AFFIRMATIONS:

God does not look at my outward appearance. He looks at my heart (1 Samuel 16:7)

PROCLAMATIONS:

The LORD opens to me His good treasure, the heavens to give the rain to my land in its season and to bless all the work of my hand (Deuteronomy 28:12).

Walk with Me Lord!

Day 2

WORD CURSES

Ephesians 4:29

Let no unwholesome word proceed from your mouth, but only such a word as is good for edification according to the need of the moment, so that it will give grace to those who hear.

DEVOTION

I can remember frequently being told I was terrible as a child by adults mainly because I was always into things. I was curious about how they worked. I didn't have faith in people, so I had to find out for myself. While riding home, I can remember one particular day on the school bus a kid offered all of the children baby aspirin. I knew what they were because my mom was a nurse; however, because no one ever listens to me and always found a way to say it was me, I never said a word. One of the children on the bus got very sick, and I can remember my grandmother asking me if I saw anyone on the bus with that aspirin and I said no. However, when she finished talking to the person who called to ask, she came to me and said, "Look at me in my face. Tell me the truth." I said, "Granny, does it matter because I'm going to be blamed anyway?" My grandmother then explained to me the importance of telling someone about the issue we see and not worry about those who blame us. She also apologized for allowing that word "bad" to become my norm to the point that it built fear. That's how the enemy gets us; he always plays with our emotions. We see this repeatedly in the Bible.

Now I know many will say well that is simple, but as adults, we hear wrong things, which are said often and never say anything. We see the mistreatment of children using profanity or word curses over them that will shape their minds for life. We assume that's not my child; let me mind my business. We see a husband talking down to his wife, and we say that's not my business. Let me keep quiet. We see pastors and teachers teaching false doctrine and stealing God's glory; we won't say a word. Instead, we use words like God will judge them, or it all comes out in the long run. Well, let me tell you, God is concerned about everything. No matter how big or small, God is concerned with the perfecting of the Body of Christ. Whether you believe it's your responsibility or not God will hold you accountable for every word spoken out of your mouth and those words we heard from others about others, but we didn't bring correction.

For that very reason, we should hold every able believer accountable while building an iron-clad foundation by being the iron to one another that sharpens according to (Proverbs 27:17) with every interaction until our Father in heaven returns.

SELF-EVALUATION

What do you hear about daily life or death?

What kind of words are coming out of your mouth, life, or death?

PRAYER

Dear Heavenly Father, I bring my brother and sister before You. Lord, I come to You glorifying You for the God that You are. Lord, I ask you to deliver my brother or sister from any wicked communication, any wicked listening, and any evil acts. Lord, I come against the enemy that has been feeding them lies. I command every silver cord to be cut and any demon back to the pits of hell where they belong. Lord, I ask You to send Your fire upon them from the top of their head to the sole of their feet. Lord, I invite You to heal itching ears in the name of Jesus. Lord, we ask You to release complete life healing and for you to pour Your spirit upon them. God, I ask all these things in your son Jesus' name, Amen.

REFLECTION:

AFFIRMATIONS:

If I don't stand firmly in my faith, I won't stand at all. (Isaiah 7:9)

PROCLAMATIONS:

I lend to many nations, but I will not borrow (Deuteronomy 28:12).

_____
_____
_____
_____
_____
_____
_____
_____
_____
_____
_____
_____
_____

GUARD OUR TONGUES

Proverb 11:9

Evil words destroy one's friends; wise discernment rescues the godly.

DEVOTION

I can remember a time when my life was complicated. God was healing my life, but before he could completely heal me, He had to work something out of me. I went through so much pain from being cheated on, being told I was stupid and that

I was good for nothing but having babies. These words plagued me. Not only did those words bring curses upon me, but I took those words to heart. We have to guard what we allow to come into our hearts. Proverb 4:23 says, "Keep thy heart with all diligence, for out of it are the issues of life ." Words are unseen chains that can bind at any given time and destroy you instantly.

Matthew 12:34 says, "You brood of vipers, how can you who are evil say anything good? For out of the overflow of the heart, the mouth speaks." Luke 6:45 says, "The good man brings good things out of the good treasure of his heart, and the evil man brings evil things out of the evil treasure of his heart. For out of the overflow of the heart, the mouth speaks."

Many people have heart issues, and they take those issues and pass them on to the next person. Or because that person is not happy with their life choices, they may attack you, but there is a God who can protect us if we don't walk in the spirit of offense. Allow Him to guard your words with grace to heal every broken heart with which you come in contact.

SELF-EVALUATION

Who are you destroying with your words, yourself, your husband, children, or the people around you?

What are your go-to words?

Do they bring freedom or display grace?

PRAYER

Dear Heavenly Father, I bring every individual reading this devotional before You. I command every broken heart, the spirit of offense, the spirit of bondage sent forth by the words of their mouths, and the mouths of others to be broken in the name of Jesus. I release 1 John 1:9 that states, "If I confess my sins, he is faithful and to forgive me of my sins and to cleanse me from all unrighteousness (Thompson, 2007)." I decree that God is making all your brokenness whole and that He brings restorations to every area of your life in the name of Jesus.

REFLECTION:

Walk with Me Lord!

AFFIRMATIONS:

God is love and he is in me, so I am love. (1 John 4:16)

Walk with Me Lord!

PROCLAMATIONS:

The Lord makes me the head and not the tail, above and not beneath (Deuteronomy 28:13).

Walk with Me Lord!

WORD BATTLE

Proverbs 15:1

A gentle answer turns away wrath, but hard words stir up anger.

DEVOTION

When we communicate every day, we are faced with the decision of how to respond. I remember once coming to my leader excited about something the Lord showed me during my prayer time. Although I was nervous, my leader became very argumentative and began to pick apart everything I was saying to tear me down. I could feel the spirit of anger trying to come upon me, but instead, I humbled myself and did what I knew to do in God's Word. Psalms 91:1 states, "He that dwelleth in the secret place of the highest shall abide under the shadow of the Almighty." I hid, which brought the protection of the Lord. I was in an attack that did not affect me because I had seen the danger. Therefore, I hid. In my hiding, I was protected not just from the words that were said but also from the enemy who loves to intensify a situation which would birth envy, strife, and anger in me. However, my soft answer allowed the Lord to move on my behalf, who vindicated me by causing that person to apologize for discouraging me from doing what the Lord was telling me to do.

SELF-EVALUATION

When you are angry, what kind of words come out of your mouth?

Are those words forgiving or unforgiving?

PRAYER

Dear Heavenly Father, we come to You asking for help with our mouths. We bind up any words that have caused anger and strife. We release the love of Christ, which covers a multitude of sins (1 Peter 4:8). Lord, help us to be able to decree when to speak and when to listen as You have directed us in James 1:19. Lord, I decree we will be swift to hear, slow to speak, and slow to wrath. I come against the spirit of fear and any other spirits that try to come upon you as your mouth comes in line with the righteousness of God. I decree the Lord is your salvation, and there are no people, places, or things to fear. I release peace, hope, and the glory of the Lord over everything the Lord has called you to do in your current season and every season to come.

REFLECTION:

AFFIRMATIONS:

When I'm distressed, I cry to God for help and he hears my voice. (Psalm 18:6)

_____

_____

_____

_____

_____

_____

_____

_____

_____

_____

_____

_____

_____

PROCLAMATIONS:

I am my Father's daughter. I am always with Him and all that He has is mine (Luke 15:31).

_____
_____
_____
_____
_____
_____
_____
_____
_____
_____
_____
_____
_____
_____

WEEKLY REVIEW

Behavior Change

Reflection Questions:

What did you learn about yourself this week?
Did you maintain any Scriptures from this week's devotionals?
If you didn't maintain any Scripture, what are you doing to ensure you do in the future?

How much time did you spend after each devotion waiting in quiet time to hear from God?

Are you journaling?

REFLECTION:

_____
_____
_____
_____
_____
_____
_____
_____
_____
_____

Walk with Me Lord!

AFFIRMATIONS:

God quiets my deep inner hunger because I am cherished by him. (Psalm 17:14)

When I cry to God for relief from the deepest pits of my life, he hears me. (Lamentations 3:55-56)

_____

_____

_____

_____

_____

_____

_____

_____

_____

_____

_____

Walk with Me Lord!

PROCLAMATIONS:

God blesses me and surrounds me with favor as a shield (Psalm 5:12).

My ways please the LORD and He makes even my enemies to be at peace with me (Proverbs 16:7).

_____

_____

_____

_____

_____

_____

_____

_____

_____

_____

_____

Walk with Me Lord!

Day 6

DECEITFUL TONGUE

Proverbs 15:4
Gentle words bring life and health; a deceitful tongue crushes the spirit.

DEVOTION

The word deceitful is defined as having a tendency or disposition to deceive or give a false impression or not honest or deceptive misleading.[6]

6. 2019 Merriam-Webster, I. (2019, May 24). Deceitful. Retrieved

Anytime you speak deceitful, misleading, or dishonest words, you are opening yourself and the (un)intended receiver up to danger. Many times, we mislead those around us because we are bound, or more concerned with our successes. Sometimes we deceive mistakenly. However, we never go back to the person and correct our mistakes once we have been made aware of the error. Which is why the unintended receiver gets hurt because we tend to repeat things as we feel it will help us. Insecurities and jealousy are a few reasons we deceive. The insecurities come because we think that the person is getting more attention or accolades, or they do something better than us. That's when anxieties arise, and we begin to act out. However, the fruit we display is of the devil instead of the fruit of the Spirit. 1 Peter 5:7 reminds us to cast all our anxieties on Him because He cares for us. The Bible tells us that the body of Christ is made of one body, but many members. Depending on our ability and willingness to be teachable, we can hinder ourselves from progressing.

---

from Merriam Webster Dictionary: https://www.merriam-webster.com/dictionary/deceitful

SELF-EVALUATION

Are you deceitful in your communication?
Are you hiding the real you behind deception?

PRAYER

Dear Heavenly Father help me to not create a false reality based on my shortcomings. Deliver me from the control of anxiety and fear. Lord allow me to recognize and know the real me. The person you have created me to be. Lord, regulate my mind so that my words will be the truth. Lord, help me to understand that the truth shall set me free and those who hear my voice. Lord, we release Psalms 145:18 in my life that reminds me that you are near to all who call on You, to all who call on You in truth. Thus, today I stand, therefore, having fastened on the belt of truth and having put on the breastplate of righteousness (Ephesians 6:14). I decree that I will no longer walk in the lies and deceit of the enemy. I decree that I will walk in truth. I decree I am fearfully and wonderfully made in the name of Jesus, Amen.

REFLECTION:

AFFIRMATIONS:

When I'm distressed, I cry to God for help and he hears my voice. (Psalm 18:6)

PROCLAMATIONS:

But by God's doing, I am in Christ Jesus. He became to me wisdom, righteousness, sanctification, and redemption (I Corinthians 1:30).

_____
_____
_____
_____
_____
_____
_____
_____
_____
_____
_____
_____
_____
_____
_____

Day 7

THOUGHTFUL WORDS

Proverb 16:24

Kind words are like honey-sweet to the soul and healthy for the body.

DEVOTION

Kindness defined as fundamental nature or quality.[7] The word thoughtful means given to

7. 2019 Merriam-Webster, I. (2019, May 24). Kind. Retrieved from Merriam Webster Dictionary: https://www.merriam-webster.com/dictionary/kind

or chosen or made with heedful anticipation of the needs and wants of others.[8] Everything about our relationship with God is about others. God Himself sent His Son to die on the cross for others like you and me (John 3:16). He did this so that you and I would be able to come before Him and be forgiven. However, this world teaches people to be only concerned with themselves and not worried if those around you are struggling. Thoughtful words can create a joyful day for someone on the verge of giving up. I can remember when I was first beginning to get serious about the things of God. Someone in my current church family asked me if I would give the Lord a try. I had accepted Christ as my savior. I had been coming to that church for a few Sundays out of duty. However, I hadn't allowed the Lord to start His process of conversion by submitting to the teaching of God's Word.

2 Timothy 2:15 says, "For us to study to shew thyself approved unto God, a workman that needeth not to be ashamed, rightly dividing the word of truth." Those words stopped me from

---

8. 2019 Merriam-Webster, I. (2019, May 24). Merriam Webster Dictionary. Retrieved from Thoughtful: https://www.merriam-webster.com/dictionary/thoughtful

being religious, which is to practice in something ritually. Those words caused me to form a lasting relationship that has changed my life. I didn't just accept Christ, but I allowed Him ultimately into my life that He may make me whole to be used for His Glory.

SELF-EVALUATION

Do you practice being concerned for others without looking for something in return?

Does your life exemplify the forgiven nature of our Lord and Savior Jesus Christ?

PRAYER

Dear Heavenly Father, I ask You to help me to consider other people when I am speaking. Help me to be concerned with my brother and sister no matter where I am or what I am doing. Help me to speak kindly, build up and not tear down. I bind up the spirit of pride, and I release humility and the love of Christ. Lord, I release every hurt that causes me to hind behind that hurt. I ask for the mind of Christ listed in Phil. 2 that I may think, speak, and be just who Christ was.

May my mouth be full of love and allow others to see Christ and not myself. I ask all these things in the name of Jesus Christ.

REFLECTION:

_____
_____
_____
_____
_____
_____
_____
_____
_____
_____
_____

Walk with Me Lord!

AFFIRMATIONS:

Because I've walked through Jesus' gate, I've found green pastures. (John 10:9)

Walk with Me Lord!

PROCLAMATIONS:

God quiets my deep inner hunger because I am cherished by him. (Psalm 17:14)

Walk with Me Lord!

LIFE-GIVING WORDS

Proverbs 18:4

A person's words can be life-giving water; words of true wisdom are as refreshing as a bubbling brook.

DEVOTION

Life-giving words bring life in a dead situation. Life-giving words can take you from a hopeless situation and breathe life into you. I can remember experiencing sickness and, in the moment, feeling hopeless. The doctors had given me no hope, and many of my family members began to push me to accept the fact my life was coming to an end. Then one day in my kitchen while making tea, I began to cry. I cried out to God and said, I don't want to die. I want to see my children grow up and see my grandchildren. I then slid down in the corner of my kitchen and sobbed as I had never cried before. Then out of nowhere, I heard a voice say, "GET UP". Those words dried my tears instantly, and once I began to stand. I felt refreshed, strengthened, and empowered. As I looked around, no one was in the room. I knew at that moment the Holy Ghost had spoken to me when no one else had words God did. Sometimes we have to look to God for our strength.

Psalms 112:1-2 says, "I will lift my eyes unto the hills, from whence cometh my help. My help cometh from the Lord, which made heaven and earth." We have to learn to depend on God for our needs. God can send impossible things to shift our lives. Thus, when you see hopelessness before you, speak God's living Word that it may create and regenerate rivers of living water that will transform your life and those around you forever.

SELF-EVALUATION

Do your words birth life to others?

Do your words birth life in yourself?

PRAYER

Dear Heavenly Father, I come to you right now, asking for your everlasting love to fall on me like never before. I come against any sickness, disease, stronghold, or curse before me and command them up and out of me and my life and back to the pits of hell where they belong. Lord, I present my life a living sacrifice holy before Your throne that it may be a living sacrifice unto you sacrificed as in Romans 12:1. I understand that the weapons of our warfare are not carnal, but mighty through God to the pulling down of strongholds as so taught by Paul in 2 Corinthians 10:4-5. Lord, I ask You to release Nehemiah 8:10 upon me that your joy will be my strength in every situation and circumstance. I take up my bed and walk according to Your Word and precepts. I ask these things in your Son Jesus' name Amen.

REFLECTION:

AFFIRMATIONS:

When I'm distressed, I cry to God for help and he hears my voice. (Psalm 18:6)

_____
_____
_____
_____
_____
_____
_____
_____
_____
_____
_____
_____
_____
_____

PROCLAMATIONS:

The God of hope fills me with all joy and peace in believing so that I abound in hope by the power of the Holy Spirit (Romans 15:13).

_____
_____
_____
_____
_____
_____
_____
_____
_____
_____
_____
_____
_____

SATISFYING WORDS

Proverbs 18:20

Words satisfy the soul as food satisfies the stomach. The right words on a person's lips bring satisfaction.

DEVOTION

The word satisfying means producing pleasure or contentment by providing what is needed or wanted.[9] A man must accept the penalties of

9. 2019 Merriam-Webster, I. (2019, May 25). Satisfying. Retrieved

his words, good or evil. The grace of God makes it easy to forgive, but our selfish corruption makes it difficult. Proverb 12 tells us the transgression of his lips snares the wicked: but the just shall come out of trouble. Out of our mouths flows the issues of life; however, if we are casting our hearts (issues) on our Father, then our words will build up and bring peace and satisfaction to all those who hear them. Think about the testimonies you have heard of those who God has delivered, healed, guided, and rescued. How did those testimonies make you feel? Did they bring hope? I know when I hear about doing the impossible, it encourages me because I know if He did it for them, He can do it for me.

Therefore, here is a testimony for you. I have had to stand in many battles. One of the greatest ones was for me, standing in the gap for my husband to become saved. Many people close to me said it couldn't be done. Even when I told them what God had promised me that if I stand, He will give him back to me. Most said that's not a word from God because the Bible says he who findeth

---

from Merriam Webster Dictionary: https://www.merriam-webster.com/dictionary/satisfying

a wife findeth a good thing. However, what they missed was that he was already my husband. He had already chosen me. Thus, I stood through all the mistreatment with affairs, neglect, belittling, and no support. Until my God, one day out of nowhere, delivered him. I knew he was delivered because he first confessed his life to Christ, then turned and fell on his knee, confessed what he had done to me, and asked me for forgiveness. I began to praise the Lord because of what He had promised me. The promise had come to the past, not in secret. But in front of all those who doubted what God had promised me he would do. Thus, I will praise Him because I understand that praise is the currency of me receiving my breakthrough. When you get in a hard place, look to those around you and ask them to share their testimonies with you that their words may bring satisfaction to your spirit, man.

SELF-EVALUATION

Are you satisfied with where God has you?
Do you understand why He has you there?
What testimonies have you seen or heard that the Lord has done in your life and others?

PRAYER

Dear Heavenly Father, I thank You for Your saving grace. I thank You for not leaving me in this world to fight my battles alone. Lord, thank You for the divine connections You have placed around me for support and help. Lord, allow me to look past my situation and focus on the mighty works I've seen You do countless times. Build my understanding that I am blessed with every spiritual blessing in Christ, as mentioned in Ephesians 1:3. Lord, help me to believe that all that You have for me will come unto me, as spoken in John 6:37. Lastly, Lord, I will praise You. I will appreciate You, for I'm fearfully and wonderfully made in You. I ask these things in Your Son Jesus' name Amen.

REFLECTION:

AFFIRMATIONS:

I have life, now & eternally, because of God's grace. It's not because of anything I have done. Eph 2:8-9

PROCLAMATIONS:

The Lord of peace is peace. In every way, He always gives me His peace (2 Thessalonians 3:16).

_____
_____
_____
_____
_____
_____
_____
_____
_____
_____
_____
_____

Day 10

WEEKLY REVIEW

Reflection Questions:

What did you learn about yourself this week?

How did you add this change to your life?

Did you maintain any Scriptures from this week's devotionals?

If you didn't maintain any Scriptures, what are you doing to ensure you do in the future?

How much time did you spend after each devotion waiting in quiet time to hear from God?

Are you journaling?

REFLECTION:

Walk with Me Lord!

AFFIRMATIONS:

The Lord stands at my side and gives me strength to share his Good News with others. (2 Timothy 4:17)

As I lose my life for Christ's sake, I find true life in him. (Matthew 10:39)

Walk with Me Lord!

PROCLAMATIONS:

I always rejoice and pray without ceasing. In everything, I give thanks for this is the will of God in Christ Jesus for me (I Thessalonians 5:16-18).

I am steadfast of mind. He keeps me in perfect peace because I trust in Him (Isaiah 26:3).

_____

_____

_____

_____

_____

_____

_____

_____

_____

_____

Walk with Me Lord!

HARMFUL WORDS

Proverbs 25:18

Telling lies about others is as harmful as hitting them with an ax, wounding them with a sword, or shooting them with a sharp arrow.

DEVOTION

The word harmful means of a kind likely to be damaging.[10] We all at one time or another have

---

10. 2019 Merriam-Webster, I. (2019, May 24). Harmful Retrieved from Merriam Webster Dictionary: https://www.merriam-webster.

lied about something. We can say that the lie was harmless or small. No matter the size, words can hurt. Do you remember the saying, "Sticks and stones can break my bones, but words will never hurt me?" That is a lie straight from the pits of hell. Words can haunt us in our sleep because we are in a quiet place. Words can follow from generation to generation. They're called 'word curses'! Saying mean and hateful things to people can destroy a person's entire life. I remember, as a child, I always got into trouble at school. The assistant principal told me directly that he hated me. I would be like 'okay', 'so' and keep doing whatever I was doing wrong. Then one day, that same principle told me if I kept behaving badly, I would fail. Not just fail, but he said, "You're going to be a teenage mom who depends on welfare and who has no other value." I think I was in the fifth grade when he said these words to me.

Jeremiah 9:8 says, "Their tongues are deadly arrows; they speak deception. With his mouth, a man speaks peace to his neighbor, but in his heart, he sets a trap for him." It wasn't until shortly after I gave my life to Christ that those

com/dictionary/harmful

words were brought back to my remembrance. I remember the Lord having me to reject those words and He told me to go forward. We have to be careful about what we say to our neighbors and their children.

SELF-EVALUATION

Are you known as the gossiper?

When information is brought to you, do you add more info based on your perception, or do you pray for the situation for God to show you what is taking place?

PRAYER

Dear Heavenly Father, I come to You right now, asking You to destroy any negative words spoken out of my mouth that birth hurt, harm, or shame. Lord, I also ask You to break off any hurt, damage, or shameful words spoken over my life. Lord, help me to release Proverbs 24:28 over my life, which directs me not to testify against my neighbor without cause and not to deceive with my lips. My words shall teach, encourage, and deliver all those who are within the sound of my voice. I request these things in your Son Jesus Holy Name, Amen.

REFLECTION:

AFFIRMATIONS:

I give my anxieties to God and know that he'll take them because he loves me. This gives me peace. 1 Peter 5:7

PROCLAMATIONS:

The joy of the LORD is my strength (Nehemiah 8:10).

MEDIATOR WORDS

Deuteronomy 5:5

I stood between the LORD and you at that time, to shew you the word of the LORD: for ye were afraid because of the fire and went not up into the mount, saying.

DEVOTION

There will be times in our lives when those around us will lack the faith to overcome situations in their life. Just as God loved the world so much, He sent His Son that we all may have the opportunity to come before the Father naked and not ashamed (John 3:16). When you see the lack, hurt, or pain in people's lives, are you putting those people before the Father? Putting them before Him asking Him to heal, deliver and set free those people. Regardless of who you are, we all called to pray. Prayer is a way to intercede for those who may be too worried to do so for themselves. As I stated previously in this devotional at one point in my life, I was severely sick with ovarian cancer. To the end that many people, including myself, thought I was going to lose my life. However, there were a few people whose faith surpassed mine and encouraged me to believe God for my healing.

Every Wednesday during Bible Study, one of those people (a woman from church) would anoint my head and pray for me. Another one of those ladies would pray with me as well. Both of these powerful women of God always reminded me that God was able to heal and deliver me out of that situation; however, I needed to trust Him. I had been saved for two years when this situation happened, now it has been many years since then and I often reflect on the fact these ladies carried me with their faith to see beyond what I could see. Matthew 17:20 states, "Because you have so little faith, answered. For truly I tell you, if you have faith the size of a mustard seed, you can say to this mountain, 'Move from here to there,' and it will move. Nothing will be impossible for you." A seed of faith was planted in me that has grown to a mustard tree that roots cover me from the top of my head to the soul of my feet.

SELF-EVALUATION

Who have you interceded for today?
Have you asked anyone to intercede on your behalf lately?

PRAYER

Dear Heavenly Father, help me to understand the importance of standing in the gap for others. Lord, please keep Your loving heart before and within me that I may practice 1 Peter 4:8, allowing the love of Christ to cover the sins of all those around me. Not to judge their acts but taking them before your thorn that you may supply every need. That I may go due as Deuteronomy 5:27 state and "Go thou near, and hear all that the LORD our God shall say: and speak thou unto us all that the LORD our God shall speak unto thee; and we will listen to it, and do it." I ask these things in your Son Jesus' name, Amen.

REFLECTION:

_____

_____

_____

_____

_____

_____

_____

_____

_____

Walk with Me Lord!

AFFIRMATIONS:

I alone am not competent. My competence comes from God. (2 Corinthians 3:5)

Walk with Me Lord!

PROCLAMATIONS:

I am confident of this very thing, that He who has begun a good work in me will complete it until the day of Jesus Christ (Philippians 1:6).

Walk with Me Lord!

WORDS EMPOWER

Proverbs 18:21

Life and death are in the power of the tongue, and those who love it will eat its fruit.

DEVOTION

The word empowerment means the state of being empowered to do something: the power, right, or authority to do something.[11]

---

11. 2019 Merriam-Webster, I. (2019, May 25). Empowerment. Retrieved from Merriam Webster Dictionary: https://www.merriam-webster.com/dictionary/empowerment

Many of us go through a time where we struggle to get up out of bed. During these times, I have had to push-pull and drag myself to get moving. Even though I knew I needed to move, my body would not listen, and I would struggle all day from my attitude to just focusing on the task that needed that day. One day during prayer, I heard the Holy Ghost say to me, "You tried your words, now use mine." These words quickened my spirit and gave me a hunger and thirst for God's Word like no other.

Matthew 5:6 states, "Blessed are they which do hunger and thirst after righteousness: for they shall be filled." The words 'blessed are' in this scripture means happy, to be envied.[12] When you get to the point that nothing else helps you to push forward, that is when you need to use the Word of the Lord to push yourself forward. Sometimes the craving of bodily hunger goes beyond natural things, and you must partake in a Biblical meal that is sure to please nourishment requirements within the body. God did not create us to abstain from His Word. His word is what

---

12. Strong LLd STD, J. (2010). Strong Exhaustive Concordance of the Bible. Nashville, TN: Thomas Nelson Publishers.

keeps us in alignment and position. To live, move and have our being within our Father in Heaven.

SELF-EVALUATION

When was the last time you partook in a spiritual meal that included reading your Bible?

In your weakest moments, what source do you depend on to help you?

EXTRA THOUGHTS

If your source is anything but Jesus Christ, then you need to reevaluate your relationship. God is our source, and everything else is our resource. Jesus is the correct solution to every problem, no matter the size or complication.

PRAYER

Dear Heavenly Father, I come to You the only way I know how emptying all that I think that I am. I put my mind, heart, and entire being in Your hands. Lord, I need You to be my strength when I'm weak. I need You to be my source of all things. Lord, I give You every fear, doubt, and want. I cast down anything I've tried to fix myself instead of trusting You. Lord, I confess my sins. You are faithful and just to forgive me my sins and to cleanse me from all unrighteousness (1 John 1:9). Today I renew my vow unto You, and I praise You for your everlasting love and compassion. Psalms 66:13 says, "I will go into thy house with burnt offerings: I will pay thee my vows. I will forever praise your name for the freedom and life you have given unto me." 1 Peter 2:9 says, "But ye are a chosen generation, a royal priesthood, a holy nation, a peculiar people; that ye should shew forth the praises of him who hath called you out of darkness into his marvelous light." I ask these things in your Son Jesus' name, Amen.

REFLECTION:

Walk with Me Lord!

AFFIRMATIONS:

God is faithful. He'll complete the good work that he has begun in me. (Philippians 1:6)

_____
_____
_____
_____
_____
_____
_____
_____
_____
_____
_____
_____
_____
_____
_____

Walk with Me Lord!

PROCLAMATIONS:

God works in me both to will and to do His good pleasure (Philippians 2:13).

Walk with Me Lord!

IDLE WORDS

Matthew 12:36

Jesus said, "I tell you that everyone will have to give account on the Day of Judgment for every empty word they have spoken."

DEVOTION

Idle words are translated to empty words in the King James Version of the Bible. I can remember when I first gave my life to Christ; I had a habit of telling myself things like, "One day I will be somebody. One day someone will love and appreciate me. One day...one day," I spoke that over my life again and again. Then one day, as I read my Bible, I came across the Scripture, 2 Corinthians 12:9 that says, "And he said unto me, My grace is sufficient for thee: for my strength is made perfect in weakness. Most gladly, therefore, will I rather glory in my infirmities, that the power of Christ may rest upon men."

As I read those words, my heart filled, and although the words said my grace is sufficient, my heart heard my love is adequate. Those words were like a bulldozer moving a cement wall that had been curing for over twenty years. What I read on that day opened up my understanding of the importance of allowing God's Word to lead my life. Then I learned of Philippians 4:13, I can do all things through Christ who gives me strength. It was like years of doubt and uncertainty came off of me as I read God's Word. Then I began to repeat those words to myself when I felt weak or worried. My words changed from being empty to being empowered with the Power of Christ to shape and turn me into who He called me to be.

SELF-EVALUATION

What type of words do you use during prayer? Are they full of substance or air?

Are your words empowering to yourself and others?

PRAYER

Dear Heavenly Father, please help me with my heaviness. Lord, I bind up my negative words and the dying words of others. Lord, I command the spirit of heaviness to come out of my body in the name of Jesus. I release the healing virtue of Christ upon me. Lord, help me to guard my gate not to receive anything that was not of You. Proverbs 10:11 says, "The mouth of the righteous is a fountain of life, but violence overwhelms the mouth of the wicked." God, I need you to help me, O Lord my God, for I rely on you (2 Chronicles 14:11). I declare that I will commit my way to the Lord, and I will trust in him, and he will act on my behalf (Psalms 37:5). Hear O Lord, and be merciful on me. O Lord, be my helper (Psalm 30:10). I declare that I'm a child of God. I declare

I have the mind of the highest God. I pray all these things in the name of Jesus Christ, Amen.

REFLECTION:

AFFIRMATIONS:

I run along the paths of God's commands because He has set my heart free. (Psalm 119:32)

PROCLAMATIONS:

I do all things without grumbling or complaining so that I will prove myself to be blameless and innocent. I am a child of God who is above reproach in the midst of a crooked and perverse generation, among whom I appear as lights in the world (Philippians 2:14-15).

Day 15

WEEKLY REVIEW

Reflection Questions:

What did you learn about yourself this week?
How did you add this change to your life?
Did you maintain any Scriptures from this week's devotionals?

If you didn't maintain any Scriptures, what are you doing to ensure you do in the future.

How much time did you spend after each devotion waiting in quiet time to hear from God?

Are you journaling?

REFLECTION:

Walk with Me Lord!

AFFIRMATIONS:

I am able to keep my ways pure, but only by living according to God's Word. (Psalm 119:9)

Walk with Me Lord!

PROCLAMATIONS:

I hold fast to the word of life. In the day of Christ's return, I will have reason to glory because I did not run or labor in vain (Philippians 2:16).

Walk with Me Lord!

Day 16

RIGHTEOUS WORDS

Proverbs 10:32
The lips of the righteous know what is fitting, but the mouth of the wicked only what is perverse.

DEVOTION

The word righteous means acting in accordance with divine or moral law: free from guilt or sin.[13] Proverbs 14:12 says, "There is a way which

13. Strong LL. D S.T.D, J. (1996). The New Strong's Complete

seemeth right unto a man, but the end thereof are the ways of death." God's way can also go beyond our way, and the words we use. Righteous words must be seasoned with grace or love. God's Word says in 1 Corinthians 13:5 that love is not rude. It doesn't insist on its way; it is not irritable or resentful. God's word also says, "Love bears all things, believes all things, hopes all things, [and] endures all things (1 Corinthians 13:7)."

We all have had a friend that does something that does not meet the standard of God. How do you handle those things? Do you attack your friend condemning them, or do you season your words with grace? Now let's go one step further. How do you deal with the shortcomings of your apostle, prophet, evangelist, pastor, or teachers or any other church leader? Do you cover them, or do you gossip about their faults? I'm not speaking to the fact you are discussing with other believers for clarity because we know sometimes you will need clarity because the enemy loves to sow discord. I'm talking about the negative talk that turns into unrighteousness. We are living in

---

Dictionary of Bible Words. Nashville, Tennessee: Thomas Nelson Publishers.

a day and age where the body of Christ is under attack. Kingdom believers must learn to hold each other up and cover each other for us to push past the warfare before us. We must love unconditionally. We must learn to be slow to judge and quick to speak righteousness to one another to bring correction and repentance. God's Word has made provisions (Matthew 18:15-17) for us if we have issues with our leaders. Let us learn to follow them that we will be found blameless before the Father.

SELF-EVALUATION

Are your lips filled with righteousness regardless of the situation before you?

Is your foundation in life based on God's system or this world's system?

PRAYER

Dear Heavenly Father, please forgive us for judging our leadership and brothers and sisters in Christ without bringing them up before You. Lord, help us to love the church as you enjoy the church. Please help us to be more understanding and caring for one another. Please help us to be bold as a lion but gentle as a lamb in any and every situation. Lord help us to understand proper order in communicating with our leadership but also to extend them grace just as grace has extended unto us. Lord soften our hearts and heal us from all church hurt. Let our tongue be restrained with truth and righteousness for your namesake. We ask these things in your Son, Jesus's name, Amen.

REFLECTION:

_____
_____
_____
_____
_____
_____

AFFIRMATIONS:

If I don't stand firmly in my faith, I won't stand at all. (Isaiah 7:9)

PROCLAMATIONS:

I always rejoice in the Lord and my gentleness (courteousness or self-control) is known to all people (Philippians 4:4,5).

Day 17

WORDS OF WISDOM

Proverb 10:31
"The mouth of the righteous brings forth wisdom, but a perverse tongue will be cut out."

DEVOTION

Every time I think of wisdom, my mind goes to King Solomon in the Bible. God offered Solomon anything he wanted, and he requested wisdom and knowledge. He didn't ask for common knowledge but the wisdom that surpasses all understanding. The wisdom that goes beyond what you see or hear. The wisdom that is handed down only through God that will guide you and all those around you beyond anything you could imagine. Wisdom is one of my greatest desires. Why, you ask? Because in this world, there are so many things that appear to be one way; however, the longer we watch them unfold, they manifest into something different. The wisdom of God helps you see ahead because you're not governed by the space in this world. You are tapped into eternity with the Father. This wisdom can save lives and help those who are existing to begin to live genuinely. Wisdom enables you to make the right decision the first time. God's Word says in Proverbs 3:13-14, "Happy is the man that findeth wisdom, and the man that getteth understanding. For the merchandise of it is better than the merchandise of silver, and the gain thereof than fine gold." Wisdom is valued over any money, property, or person. We should all strive for wisdom and understand that we might bring light to this world of God's trues on a higher level.

SELF-EVALUATION

Are you seeking Godly Wisdom?
If you said yes, how are you seeking it?
Are your words laced with the wisdom of God or the knowledge of this world system?

PRAYER

Dear Heavenly Father, I repent for anything that I have put in place of Your revelatory wisdom. Lord, I repent for depending on this world for my knowledge and understanding instead of You. I bind up any false knowledge or understanding that I have created laws in my heart upon, and I cast them up and out. I release your wisdom and knowledge upon me from your Word. That my ears will crave your truths, and my tongue will speak wisdom like never before. I guard my gates, which are my eyes, ears, and mouth that they will be set apart for Your use and Your use alone. I die unto myself that I may live in You. Lord, I give you full reign in my life. I love you, Lord, for You knew I found understanding and knowledge. Lord, I love you because you never leave me lost, but you continually show me yourself. I decree

I will trust the Lord with all my heart and not lean on my understanding. I decree the fear of the Lord is instructions in wisdom, and humility comes before honor. I speak all these things in your Son Jesus Holy name, Amen.

REFLECTION:

_____
_____
_____
_____
_____
_____
_____
_____
_____

Walk with Me Lord!

AFFIRMATIONS:

I am a new person, complete in Christ. (2 Corinthians 5:17)

Walk with Me Lord!

PROCLAMATIONS:

I am anxious for nothing, but in everything by prayer and supplication with thanksgiving, I let my requests be made known to God. And the peace of God, which surpasses all comprehension, will guard my hearts and minds in Christ Jesus (Philippians 4:6-7).

_____

_____

_____

_____

_____

_____

_____

_____

_____

_____

_____

Day 18

PRAYER LIFE BUILDS RIGHT WORDS

Hebrews 5:7

During the days of Jesus' life on earth, He offered up prayers and petitions with fervent cries and tears to the one who could save Him from death, and He was heard because of His reverent submission.

DEVOTION

Prayer is vital to the believer's survival. Let me repeat that prayer is essential to the believer's survival. If you are a Christian and you never take time to pray, then you are in a blind relationship with Christ. Even while Jesus was on this earth and in this earthly body, He prayed for assistance from the Father. If Jesus, the Son of the all-powerful God, prayed then we know we need to pray that the Lord will keep and guide us in the world. God says in Romans 12:2, "And be not conformed to this world: but be ye transformed by the renewing of your mind, that ye may prove what that good is, and acceptable, and perfect, will of God."

Your mind cannot be transformed if you're not in constant communication with the Father. How will you know the will of the Father for your life if you don't ask or listen to His reply? Many believers are in a nonexistent relationship. I say nonexistent because we are created in His image like Genesis 1:27 states, "So God created man in his image, in the image of God created he him; male and female created him them." Then we know that the entire design is compatible with the

Father, and if we don't like a relationship with communication, neither does our all-knowing God. Yes, He created you and saw and knows all, but as the creation, it's your duty to discuss everything about yourself with Him. Most of us have been in a relationship with the opposite sex. How did you feel when your spouse didn't communicate with you? I can tell you as a woman, I would be upset. If I hear things concerning my spouse from others, this makes me very upset. If I'm in a committed relationship, and he is the head of my household. I need to know what my husband is thinking and doing. Why? Because God didn't call me to sit and watch me being next to my husband but to hold him up in prayer daily. Early on in my marriage, it took my husband a while to get that. However, it wasn't long before he understood and came to me with everything going on with him. Our Father is concerned about us. Therefore, open up your mouth and communicate from Him, and don't forget to wait for Him to respond to you.

SELF-EVALUATION

Do you pray daily for yourself and others?

Do you wait after prayer to receive feedback from God?

Do you write down the messages received from God?

PRAYER

Dear Heavenly Father, I come to You right now, asking You to lead and guide me in my prayers. I submit my will and ways unto You and lay down everything I think I am. God says, "If I abide in you and my words abide in you and whatever I ask, it will be done," according to John 15:7. Lord, I need Your Spirit to help me when I'm weak, like, according to Romans 8:26. Lord, I will lead all my prayers like the prayer in Matthew 6:9-13: Our Father which art in heaven, Hallowed be thy name. Thy Kingdom comes, they will be done on earth, as it is in Heaven. Give us this day our daily bread. And forgive us our debts, as we forgive our debtors. And lead us not into temptation but deliver us from evil: For thine is the kingdom and the power, and the glory, forever. Amen.

REFLECTION:

Walk with Me Lord!

AFFIRMATIONS:

God forgives my wrongdoings and never remembers my sins. (Hebrews 8:12)

Walk with Me Lord!

PROCLAMATIONS:

I choose to meditate on anything that has virtue or is praiseworthy. I think about things that are true, noble, just, pure, lovely, and of good report (Philippians 4:8).

Walk with Me Lord!

Day 19

QUICK AND POWER WORDS

Hebrews 4:12

For the Word of God is living and powerful, and sharper than any two-edged sword, piercing even to the division of soul and spirit, and joints and marrow, and is a discerner of the thoughts and intents of the heart

DEVOTION

The Word of God is alive! Let me repeat that for you. The Word of God is alive! It is sharper than any spiritual weapon you can use. This weapon doesn't just shift the natural but spirit and soul. 2 Corinthians 10:4 states, "For the weapons of our warfare are not carnal, but mighty through God to the pulling down of the strongholds." Using God's Word, you pull down any high place within your life, self-exhausted or demonically controlled. The world will break that force that you can begin to govern yourself as God ordained for your life. There may be a time when the Word pierces you for perfection that you may one day be of use unto the Father in Heaven.

The Word also helps you discern things accurately around you. The more you eat of God's Word, the more you will be able to recognize what spirit is operating around you. You can be seated in a service and someone is teaching, and you will be able to determine if they are teaching from the Word, Spirit, or flesh. You may also pick up demonic activity. This will not be a time to panic but activate the Word in you and cast anything not of God down. Not just for yourself but for those around you. Don't go calling people out to their face, but call them out before the Father so that they will get free and turn back unto the Father in heaven.

The Word of God will help you to hear clearer when those around you curse you or themselves. As previously discussed in this devotional, word curses can stop, block, and hinder your movement in Christ. Thus, the more Word you know, the more you can even pick up on when someone is cursing you, but they are not using negative words. However, your discernment will be able to determine the spirit behind any words given.

The Word of God also helps you hear life issues that come out your mouth and other people's mouths. When your spirit is quickening at first, you will catch yourself saying mean things to yourself. You will have to pray to God that He will change your language to always speak life to yourself. Many of us sleep on the Word of God. We read the Bible, but we don't eat it. The Scripture tells us the Word will never return void. However, we avoid the Word of God altogether. That changes for you today.

SELF- EVALUATION

Do you read your Word?
Do you remember what you read?
Are you meditating on Scripture daily?

PRAYER

Dear Heavenly Father, thank You for being a loving God. Lord, help me to have a desire to read your Word. Lord, help me to digest your Word that the Holy Spirit will be able to bring it back to my remembrance. Lord, help me to walk in power and authority using Your Word to build up myself, my peers, and leadership. Help me to hear the spirit behind every word received that I would know what to reject and what to maintain. Lord, help me to see what is in me blocking your expression. Please help me to heal that I will be used for You one day. I ask all these things in Jesus' name, Amen.

REFLECTION:

Walk with Me Lord!

Affirmations:

I don't hide my light under a basket. I let it shine for all to see so everyone will praise my Father. (Matthew 5:15-16)

Walk with Me Lord!

Proclamations:

God instructs me and keeps me as the apple of His eye (Zechariah 2:8).

Day 20

WEEKLY REVIEW

Reflection Questions:

What did you learn about yourself this week?

How did you add this change to your life?

Did you maintain any Scriptures from this week's devotionals?

If you didn't maintain any Scriptures, what are you doing to ensure you do in the future?

How much time did you spend after each devotion waiting in quiet time to hear from God?

Are you journaling?

REFLECTION:

AFFIRMATIONS:

Because I feed on bread that comes from heaven (Jesus) I have life and live eternally. (John 6:57-58)

I give thanks to God because he is good, and his love endures forever. (Jeremiah 33:11)

_____
_____
_____
_____
_____
_____
_____
_____
_____
_____
_____

PROCLAMATIONS:

I am a crown of glory and a royal diadem in the hand of the LORD (Isaiah 62:3).

I am no longer called, forsaken or desolate. My new names are Hephzibah (my delight is in her) and Beulah (married). He delights in me and I am married to Him (Isaiah 62:4)!

_____

_____

_____

_____

_____

_____

_____

_____

_____

Day 21

PURE WORD

Proverbs 30:5
Every word of God is pure; He is a shield to those who put their trust in Him.

DEVOTION

The Word of God is pure. Perfect words for any occasion birth the perfect fruit. Producing love, joy, peace, longsuffering, gentleness, goodness, faith, meekness, temperance. The perfect fruit that develops a full spiritual life is sustained through the believer's walks thriving in humility and grace. Walking upright before the Lord awaiting His return in faith with no regret, guilt, or shame for only those with a pure heart shall see the Lord (Matthew 5:8). You have chosen purity; thus, you can show yourself to the absolute. Not pure in the flesh but rich in spirit. A pure spirit governs with full authority and power to overtake the enemies camp that the Lord be glorified among us all. Not just being a hearing but now partaking in doing what the Word says births everlasting promise to reach many of your family's generations to come.

SELF- EVALUATION

Do you examine your heart daily?

Once you find something wrong in the heart, do you bring it before the Father?

Are you practicing having a clean heart and a forgiving spirit every hour of the day?

PRAYER

Dear Heavenly Father, the only true and living God. I bring my heart before you. Lord, if there is anything unclean within my heart, I repent for it right now. Lord, if I have unforgiveness in my heart, bring it forward, and You may have it. Lord, soften my heart to love as your Son loves and to hate the things you hate. Bring anything within my heart I haven't given unto You, and I give You permission to take every evil fruit within my heart and replace it with the fruit of the spirit in Galatians 5:22. Lord, deposit a deep love in my heart for myself and others that I will love them as You loved us. I ask all these things in Jesus' name, Amen.

REFLECTION:

AFFIRMATIONS:

Experiencing God and His truths, not knowledge about Him and them, gives me abundant LIFE. (John 17:3)

Walk with Me Lord!

PROCLAMATIONS:

God rejoices over me as a bridegroom rejoices over his bride (Isaiah 62:5).

Walk with Me Lord!

Day 22

WORDS THAT STAND FOREVER

Isaiah 40:8
The grass withers, the flower fades, But the word of our God stands forever.

DEVOTION

The Words that we say daily should be a word that can stand forever. God's Word will stand the test of time. It will not wither and never fade. It holds today, yesterday and forever. The Word of God is the statue of truth for this world and the spiritual world around us. Psalms 119:89 says, "It was settled in heaven before the earth was ever formed that God's word was truth forever." Matthew and Peter both wrote about this assuring us that the Word will endure all and never fade. Therefore, it is an iron-clad weapon that can never be destroyed. It is a sword of ages created with metal, not of this world. Designed to overthrow anyone, within this earth. Above this earth or beneath the earth, that tried to refute its truth.

The Word was written for our protection so that we could search ourselves to find the truth. The Word of God has so many hidden facts that we have not even begun to discover. It is the Holy Spirit that reveals truth; therefore, we have to search diligently until we find these truths. These truths won't just shape our lives, but all those who we teach and preach to because God is not a respecter of persons, He will use anyone He chooses. I challenge you to read and study the Word more. If you practice it daily, it will become a practice that will be perfect in your life, aligning you up with how God designed us to be. We must be in constant fellowship with Him as He shapes mold and introduces new things to us as we seek His word with Him.

SELF- EVALUATION

Do you read God's Word daily?
Do you remember yesterday's Scripture?
If you answered no, go back and meditate on that word.

PRAYER

Dear Heavenly Father, thank You for Your perfect Word. Help me to allow Your Word to be hidden in my heart. Please help me to hunger for your Word daily being unsatisfied and wanting more. Please help me to apply Your divine Word to every aspect of my life. Thank you for loving us and leaving Your Word that we would have a truth to lean on at all times. Please help me to rightly divide Your Word in my life and others' life. Please help me to allow the liberties of Your Word to stand and for me not to use Your Word to manipulate and confuse the people You are calling into Your fold. Lord, I thank You for the health promises, longevity, and love obtained through Your Word. Lord, I thank You for all You have set in motion for my life, and I ask all these things in Your Son Jesus' name, Amen.

REFLECTION:

_____
_____
_____
_____
_____
_____
_____
_____
_____
_____
_____
_____

AFFIRMATIONS:

The Holy Spirit helps me understand and leads me to God's truth when I read the Bible. (John 16:12)

PROCLAMATIONS:

The LORD has chosen me for Himself as His special treasure (Psalm 135:4).

FIRE & HAMMER WORDS

Jeremiah 23:29
"Is not My word like a fire?" says the Lord,
"And like a hammer that breaks the rock in pieces?

DEVOTION

The Word of God is FIRE! Every work we perform will be tried through the Fire to determine the motive behind the spiritual work performed.

This test is before us. However, now we have an opportunity to let the FIRE of God cleanse us and purify us that our actions will be sure that when we are tested, they will come out as gold (1Corinthans 3:13). If your work is built upon the foundation of the Word, you will be rewarded; however, anything not built upon the foundation will be utterly destroyed. Which is why I love this Scripture. The Fire is for you and me to cleanse us but also to indwell us with authority and power to do more excellent works. The hammer is also multifaceted, bringing personal protection to those who attack us and also help to destroy walls that try to isolate or even hinder us. This hammer is found about six times within the Bible. It is no ordinary hammer, but one of justice and peace that is swiftly permanent to help us in every form needed.

SELF- EVALUATION

Have you experienced the Fire before? No, then request the Fire of God to fall on you now.

FIRE – FIRE - Consuming Fire, Lord consume me!

Have you called on the hammer to clear the path before you?

Hammer of the Lord - Hammer of the Lord - Move every wall - Move those Walls!

PRAYER

Dear Heavenly Father, thanks for providing weapons for our protection and cleansing for perfections. Lord, send your Fire upon me that I would be consumed in my heart, mind, and soul. Fresh Fire come! Cleanse me for Your use. Fresh Fire come! Send Your hammer to clear my path and destroy every enemy that is trying to hinder me. May your hammer guard me, smashing everything that rises above the Word of the Lord. Thank you, Lord, for the fresh Fire. Thank You for the hammer and hedge of protection. I glorify You for all You do for me. There is none higher than You, Lord, and I ask all these things in Your Son Jesus name, Amen.

REFLECTION:

Walk with Me Lord!

AFFIRMATIONS:

I am experiencing my Life as Jesus intended (1 John 5:12).

PROCLAMATIONS:

I speak God's word and hearing the word increases my faith (Romans 10:17).

Walk with Me Lord!

Day 24

BORN AGAIN WORDS

1 Peter 1:23

Having been born again, not of corruptible seed but incorruptible, through the word of God which lives and abides forever.

DEVOTION

Using words like born again is another form of purity. These words bring hope, belief, faith, obedience, love for the church, and brotherly love that creates regeneration. By purifying your soul with truth with being born again brings a newness like never before. This cleansing is necessary for those who have never been born again. Those who have to backslide and those who are still in need of deliverance. To clarify, we all stand in the need of deliverance daily for the Word says that deliverance is the children's bread. We eat bread daily; thus, we should eat God's Word daily, helping us to reject anything that is a contradiction to the Word. We use this same concept for our brothers through loving them. We display love even during fault that we may not be judged as we judge others or the measure that we use against others be used against us. Show consistent mercy that it shall be constant with you. These acts regenerate because love covers a multitude of sins, and love can be seen by all in its purest form. This is the same love Christ had when He was on the cross for all of us. This love enabled us to be born again with a new perspective according to spiritual truth. Take this truth and transform your life.

SELF- EVALUATION

Have you been born again? (If your answer is no, please go down to the salvation prayer.)

Are you still struggling with purity, and have you researched with your word what that truly means?

Do you exercise love by being your brother or sister keeper? How have you displayed this?

PRAYER

Salvation

Dear Heavenly Father,

I bring_____ before You. They are acknowledging they need a savior. They believe you are the only true living God. Right now, they put all their sins before You asking to be cleansed and made whole.

Dear Heavenly Father, thank You for everything You do for me. Lord, I come before You and ask You to search my heart, and if anything is found, not of you cleanse my soul. Lord, touch my mind that I may think clearer and carry out everything You have called me to do. Lord, deliver me from any emotional, trauma, pain, neglect, abandonment or rejection that could hinder me from moving forward in You. I don't just want to profess I am saved, but I want to be a doer of the Word as well. Lord, help me to go with You at all times, hating what You hate and loving what You love. I ask all these things in Jesus' name, Amen.

REFLECTION:

_____

_____

_____

_____

_____

_____

_____

AFFIRMATIONS:

God's Spirit in me is greater than any other spirit in the world. He enables me to live a victorious life (1 John 4:4).

PROCLAMATIONS:

I decree I am who God's Word says I am, what I have, and what I can do in Christ Jesus who gives me strength. I am established as His daughter in all ways and I shine in His light (Job 22:8, Isaiah 60:1).

Day 25

WEEKLY REVIEW

Reflection Questions:

What did you learn about yourself this week?
How did you add this change to your life?
Did you maintain any Scriptures from this week's devotionals?
If you didn't maintain any Scriptures, what are you doing to ensure you do in the future.
How much time did you spend after each devotion waiting in quiet time to hear from God?

Are you journaling?

REFLECTION:

___

AFFIRMATIONS:

More than anything else, I try to guard my heart because it determines how I live life (Proverbs 4:23).

I don't act inconsiderately but try to understand what the Lord wants me to do (Ephesians 5:17).

_____

_____

_____

_____

_____

_____

_____

_____

_____

_____

_____

Walk with Me Lord!

PROCLAMATIONS:

I speak God's Word and His angels do the voice of His Word (Psalm 103:20).

I speak God's Word and it does not return to Him void. His Word accomplishes what He pleases, and it prospers in the thing for which He sends it (Isaiah 55:11).

_____

_____

_____

_____

_____

_____

_____

_____

_____

_____

_____

Day 26

HEAVENLY WORDS

2 Peter 3:5

For this, they willfully forget that by the word of God the heavens were of old, and the earth standing out of the water and in the water.

DEVOTION

Many Christians today know everything about all the going and comings of this world but hardly anything about things concerning God's truths.

Ignorance keeps us in bondage because we have no clue of our entitlements. Kingdom believers can have any one of the three forms of ignorance: man, spiritual and God. The Bible tells us that people perish for a lack of knowledge (Hosea 4:6). As Kingdom believers, we must study everything we can to obtain what God has for us. The ignorance of man informs of the briefness of life and the limits to gain knowledge within that short time frame (Job 8:9) and our unknown future (Ecclesiastes 3:6) that we must seek out while in relationship with God. Man's ignorance also includes coming evil unforeseen (Ecclesiastes 9:12), life mysterious (Ecclesiastes 11:5), and lastly, nature and grace full of mysteries (John 3:8). All of these things concerning man are important to know to succeed as aliens of this natural world.

Another form of ignorance is of the Kingdom believers struggle with is spiritual ignorance. We must gain understanding concerning spiritual matters if you plan to walk in authority available by being in a relationship with God. It is Jesus who sends the Comforter to us that we may gain a spiritual connection to go beyond what we think like a man. God's righteousness and our willingness to be obedient unto His righteousness give us full access to spiritual things. Isaiah 1:3 states, "The ox knows its owner and the donkey its master's crib, but Israel does not know, my people do not understand.[14]" The last ignorance many believers have is ignorance of God. The creation does not understand the creator. That knowledge alone will allow that believer to gain access that others will not be able to because you know God. Several Scriptures discuss how many ignored how God works and what hinders them the most. A few for you to study are Jude 2:10, Jeremiah 4:22, Jeremiah 8:7, and Acts 17:23. To know God is to know Him. To see the Spirit is to understand the power contained within you. To know yourself is to understand the real you brighter than ever before.

SELF- EVALUATION

What have you learned concerning the ignorance of man?

What have you learned concerning the ignorance of spirit?

14. Gateway, B. (2020, February 23). Isaiah 1:3 ESV. Retrieved from Bible Gateway: https://www.biblegateway.com/passage/?search=Isaiah+1%3A3+&version=ESV

What have you learned concerning the ignorance of God?

What have you learned about the real you?

PRAYER

Dear Heavenly Father, You are the God that knows all things and holds all wisdom. Help me, Lord, to walk in Your ways. Please help me to gain knowledge and not worldly understanding. Lord open my mind to understand the things about me so that I can maneuver quicker around items that can hinder my life. Allow the Holy Spirit to teach me His ways and forever be my guide. Lord, I need You to expand my knowledge that I may unlearn bad behaviors and lead others to understand that they can grow as well. I thank You for what You are doing in my life, seen and unseen. I love You, and I ask all these things in Jesus' name, Amen.

REFLECTION:

AFFIRMATIONS:

I'm like a tree planted by streams of water. My life bears fruit and prospers because I meditate on God's Word (Psalm 1:1-2).

Walk with Me Lord!

PROCLAMATIONS:

I will speak God's Word until it accomplishes its purpose. It is like fire. It is like a hammer that shatters a rock (Jeremiah 23:29).

Walk with Me Lord!

Day 27

SWEET WORDS

Psalms 119:103

How sweet are Your words to my taste, Sweeter than honey to my mouth!

DEVOTION

We've been dealing with all types of Bible words until this point; let us take a look at sweet words. Sweet words can encourage, bring joy, and even stop strife. Our words can help the person digest difficult conversations, which can make a difference in accepting and rejecting deliverance. Think about all the times when some used pleasant words with you. These words sometimes became the foundational point of the way you treat others today. Not only that, you keep those things close to your heart to reflect on during hard times in your life. Which highlights even greater importance of our word because they are food not to the physical body but the soul. If the soul is hungry, you can hear the person lash out and lack compassion. This compassion is not our usual element of kindness, but those born through the Word of God, cleansing your heart and shaping your emotions to the correct alignment.

Deuteronomy 8:3 states, "So He humbled you, allowed you to hunger, and fed you with manna which you did not know nor did your fathers know, that He might make you know that man shall not live by bread alone, but man lives by every word that proceeds from the mouth of the Lord." God's Word gives you manna, which is food from on high that can heal, deliver, and work miracles all during digestion. These words are sweet and a treat that keeps giving that you will see the change instant in your life that you can move forward and be generous to others. You will become a sweet treat to all who hear the words out of your mouth cover in sugar.

SELF-EVALUATION

Are your words sweet or sour?

Are you unsure? Pay attention to those with whom you talk. How do they respond to you?

What are you putting in place to lead with the sweet word even in difficult times?

PRAYER

Dear Heavenly Father, thank You for your sweet words unto us as being our perfect example. Help me to see the importance of knowing Your promises that those kind words will flow through me for others and myself. Lord, help me to deal with my sharp tongue to not tear down others but to build them up. Help me not to have a sharp tongue in anger, strife, rejection, or even against those who backbite against me. Give me a forgiving heart that hurt will roll off like water. Lord, I repent for any word curses I've sent to others out of pain. Lord, I send the love of Christ upon them. I thank You for what You have done in Jesus' name, Amen.

REFLECTION:

_____
_____
_____
_____
_____
_____
_____
_____
_____
_____
_____

AFFIRMATIONS:

God's Holy Spirit, who lives in me, opens my mind to the deep truths in God's Word (1 John 2:27).

PROCLAMATIONS:

The Lord has given me the tongue of the disciples. I know how to speak a word in due season to those who are weary (Isaiah 50:4).

HEARING WORDS

Revelations 1:3
Blessed is he who reads and those who hear the words of this prophecy and keep those things which are written in it; for the time is near.

DEVOTION

The words we hear can have a positive or negative impact. The negative word can cause trauma, frustration, anger, strife, bitterness, and so much more. All of these negative attributes can cause long- and short-term harm if not properly cast upon the Lord. Positive words, like I love you, good job, well done, I'm so thankful for you are words that can help a failing heart to trust and believe again. These words can change a mindset, mend a heart, or even encourage someone. Since we are not in control of other people's mouths, we must learn to guard our ears. That they will not take in seeds of destruction. The destructive seed lays waiting to be pulled on by the enemy to torment us in our weakest hour. Therefore, we must give every evil word spoken to us and over us to God. Sometimes we must separate from those who are causing us harm that we may survive beyond the trap set for us by the enemy. Always remember the Lord will give you a way; thus, there is nothing to fear. There is only faith to gain as you learn how to walk away. We must guard and protect our ears by constantly digesting God's Word by reading and listening to the audio of the Bible every opportunity we can.

SELF- EVALUATION

How do you guard your ears?

What do you do after receiving negative words?

Do you let them lay, or do you cast them upon the Lord by praying His Word?

PRAYER

Dear Heavenly Father, thank You for being a protector of all things. Thank You for the Word You left that we all would have the most excellent tool to withstand the enemy. Please help me to guard my ears and what I allow in. Increase my discernment of things sent to cause me harm. I curse every word curse spoken over me. Lord, send the Holy Fire to freshen and renew me. I ask all these things in Jesus' name, Amen.

REFLECTION:

AFFIRMATIONS:

My faith, that saves and transforms me, comes by reading and understanding God's Word (Romans 10:12)

PROCLAMATIONS:

The Lord God awakens me every morning to fellowship with Him, and He opens my ears to hear as the learned (Isaiah 50:4).

SEED PRODUCING WORDS

Luke 8:11

Now the parable is this: The seed is the word of God.

DEVOTION

There are over sixty-six packs of seeds in the Holy Bible. The King James Authorized Bible has 783,137 words (Counter, 2020). That is over

783,137 seeds. With that vast number of seeds anyone who chooses to allow those seeds to take root within them shall have a harvest. These seeds bring a crop that no man can measure. They take every lasting root that is nurtured by the Holy Spirit to produce a sustained life that gives Glory to the Lord. These seeds build confidence, shape our future, and even help us to help others to come unto the Father. The seed from the Word of God produces much fruit. Fruit that has seeds can be replanted to regenerate. Regenerating fruit over and over because of the anointing power of the cross. We must take these seeds and plant them in our life by reading God's Word as often as we can. Not just reading but meditating and digesting His Word that we can obtain the harvest that was promised before we were ever placed in our mother's womb. A life harvest that is designed to represent the Kingdom of God at all times as we influence the entire word.

SELF- EVALUATION

How many books of the Bible have you read?
How many verses have you memorized?

The more Word in you, the higher the Holy Ghost can use you!

PRAYER

Dear Heavenly Father, thank You for giving words to my brothers and sisters within the Bible that they would scribe the information to be shared forever and ever. Lord, help my mind as I read the Bible to comprehend every word. Help me to study to show myself approved unto You and not man. Lord, water every seed planted in me that a harvest will spring up that will be fruitful and contain a seed that can continuously regenerate fruit all the days of my life. God, thank You for all You have done for me. I am forever grateful to You, and I ask all these things in your son Jesus' name, Amen.

REFLECTION:

AFFIRMATIONS:

When I humble myself before God in prayer, he hears me, and I gain understanding (Daniel 10:12).

PROCLAMATIONS:

I speak pleasant words that are sweet to the soul and healing to the bones. I am wise and I bring healing (Proverbs 16:24, Proverbs 12:18).

WEEKLY REFLECTION

Reflection Questions:

What did you learn about yourself this week?

Did you maintain any Scriptures from this week's devotionals?

If you didn't maintain any Scriptures, what are you doing to ensure you do in the future?

How much time did you spend after each devotion waiting in quiet time to hear from God?

Are you journaling?

REFLECTION:

AFFIRMATIONS:

Because I seek the Lord with all my heart, I lack no good thing (Psalm 34:10).

The key to my fruit-bearing life is hearing God's truth and understanding it (Matthew 13:23).

_____
_____
_____
_____
_____
_____
_____
_____
_____
_____
_____
_____

PROCLAMATIONS:

As I speak God's word, He sends it to heal and deliver me from my destruction (Psalm 107:20).

God redeems my life from the pit. He crowns me with loving kindness and compassion (Psalm 103:4).

_____
_____
_____
_____
_____
_____
_____
_____
_____
_____
_____
_____
_____

Walk with Me Lord!

Closing Notes

All of these things, I used to create a Godly life that is centered around Christ and who He has called me to be. Everything changes when you allow God to change your mind. I pray your mind is renewed and that you studied and journaled your renewed thought for reflection as continued edification as you walk with Christ. I've also included some of my personal proclamations and affirmations. Use these decrees and declarations to speak over your life.

Romans 4:17

"As it is written, I have made thee a father of many nations, before him whom he believed, even God, who quickened the dead, and calleth those things which be not as though they were."

PERSONAL PROCLAMATION:

I am kind and tenderhearted to others. I forgive them as God in Christ has forgiven me (Ephesians 4:32).

I can do all things through Christ who strengthens me (Philippians 4:13).

I ask God to set a guard over my mouth. He keeps watch over the door of my lips (Psalm 141:3).

I let the peace of Christ rule in my heart. As a member of one body, I am called to peace and I am thankful (Colossians 3:15 NIV).

I walk in a manner worthy of the Lord, pleasing Him in all respects. I bear fruit in every good work and I am increasing in the knowledge of God (Colossians 1:10 NAS).

I am being strengthened with all power according to His might. I have great endurance and patience (Colossians 1:11 NIV).

God has not given me a spirit of fear. He gives me power, love, and self-discipline (2 Timothy 1:7 ESV).

God loads me daily with benefits. He is my salvation (Psalm 68:19).

I am God's servant and He takes pleasure in my prosperity (Psalm 35:27).

I meditate on God's word day and night. I am successful and prosperous (Psalm 1:2-3, Joshua 1:8).

_____

_____

_____

_____

Walk with Me Lord!

PERSONAL PROCLAMATION CONTINUED:

God makes all grace abound toward me so that I always have all sufficiency and an abundance for every good work (2 Corinthians 9:8).

I honor the Lord with my wealth and the first fruits of all my produce. Then, my barns will be filled with plenty. My vats will overflow with new wine (Proverbs 3:9-10).

I bring the whole tithe into the storehouse. He opens the windows of heaven for me and pours out a blessing so great that I don't have enough room for it (Malachi 3:10).

I prosper in all things. I remain in health just as my soul prospers (3 John 1:3).

God abundantly blesses my provision (Psalm 132:15).

I give and I receive. Good measure, pressed down, shaken together, running over, will it be put into my lap (Luke 6:38).

Jesus Christ is generous in grace. Though He was rich, yet for my sake, he became poor, so that by His poverty He could make me rich (2 Corinthians 8:9).

Christ redeemed me from the curse of the law by becoming a curse for me (Galatians 3:13 NIV).

PERSONAL PROCLAMATION CONTINUED:

I experience all blessings as I obey the Lord my God (Deuteronomy 28:2 NLT).

_____

_____

_____

_____

_____

_____

_____

_____

_____

PERSONAL PROCLAMATION CONTINUED:

I am blessed in the city and blessed in the country (Deuteronomy 28:3).

I am blessed from the fruit of my body. I am blessed with today's equivalent of the produce of the ground, the increase of my herds, my cattle, and the offspring of my flock (Deuteronomy 28:4).

My kneading bowl and basket are blessed. It is the means by which I am tangibly increasing (Deuteronomy 28:5).

I am blessed when I come in and blessed when I go out (Deuteronomy 28:6).

The LORD causes my enemies who rise against me to be defeated before my face; they come out against me one way and flee before me seven ways (Deuteronomy 28:7).

The LORD commands His blessing on my storehouses and in all that I set my hand to do, and He blesses me in the land that He is giving me (Deuteronomy 28:8).

The Lord has established me as a holy person to Himself. I keep His commandments and walk in His ways (Deuteronomy 28:9).

All the people of the earth see that I am called by the name of the LORD. (Deuteronomy 28:10)

The LORD grants me plenty of goods, in the fruit of my body, in the increase of my livestock, and in the produce of my ground (Deuteronomy 28:11).

_____

_____

_____

_____

_____

_____

_____

_____

_____

Walk with Me Lord!

PERSONAL AFFIRMATIONS:

I can see the Kingdom of God because I am born again (John 3:3)

I don't worry about everyday life. God knows my needs and meets them because I make His Kingdom my primary concern (Matthew 6:25-33)

Jesus shows himself to me because I love him (John 14:21)

Because Jesus died for my sins, I am no longer separated from God. I live in close union with him (Romans 5:10)

The fruit I produce brings great joy to God, my Father in Heaven (John 15:8)

God's power works best in my weakness (2 Corinthians 12:9)

Through the energy of Christ working powerfully in me, I teach others His truths (Colossians 1:29)

Walk with Me Lord!

I have been saved, not by works, but grace, so that I might do good works (Ephesians 2:9-10)

My faith makes me whole in spirit, soul, and body (Mark 5:34)

When I call out to God, He answers me. He tells me things I wouldn't know otherwise (Jeremiah 33:3)

Because I place my hope in the Lord, my strength is renewed (Isaiah 40:31)

As I follow Jesus as I walk with him, I have peace (Luke 24:36)

Because I obey Jesus, I remain in his love (John 15:10)

The cross of Christ is my power (1 Corinthians 1:17)

My God meets all my needs (Philippians 4:19)

God is my refuge and strength always ready to help me in times of trouble (Psalm 46:1).

God gives me strength when I am weary and increases my power when I am weak (Isaiah 40:29).

About the Author

Zolisha L Ware gave her life to Christ at age 26 just a few weeks short of her 27th birthday on August 28, 2004. Zolisha has been a member of Integrity Deliverance Ministry since that date. It wasn't long after giving her life to Christ, she received the gift of the Holy Ghost during the church's 9th-anniversary service. Zolisha became the Praise & Worship Leader for the ministry in April 2005. She has continued to hold that role still today. Sometime after being made the Praise & Worship Leader, she was also charged to lead the Dance Ministry within the church.

Zolisha believes her most prized possession is her relationship unto the Lord, and you can see the evidence within her singing and dancing unto the Lord.

Before a relationship with the Lord, Zolisha was robbed of her education by anger and bitterness due to life's struggles of being a teenage mother. However, once she became under the healing power of Jesus Christ, the spirit of the Lord directed Zolisha in 2007 to pursue her education. Shortly after the ushering of the Spirit of the Lord to get her education, Zolisha found out that she should have already received her high school diploma. However, since it was so many years after that period, Zolisha was required to take two online tests: one which was within English and the other within Science to receive a fully accredited high school diploma. I am glad to report she completed both tests online quickly. After completing the classes, Zolisha was awarded her High School diploma in September 2007 from Excel High School located in Plymouth, MN. Once she was able to accomplish her high school diploma, she was continually driven by the Spirit of the Lord to further her education by signing up for college. Therefore, in the spring of 2008, Zolisha began to attend Lincoln College-Normal located. She received her Associates in Arts in 2011, and three years later, she received her Bachelors in Liberal Arts. Once Zolisha obtained her Bachelor's Degree, she thought she had completed her studies; however, the drive for education continued to burn heavily within her. Therefore, after consulting with the Lord, she enrolled in Liberty University located in Lynchburg VA in August of 2014. A year or so after being enrolled within the Master's program in May of 2015, Zolisha encountered a supernatural dream that lasted for three nights. Within that dream, Zolisha was tested on things that the Lord had delivered her from like greed, anger, sexual immorality, hate, and perversion.

At the end of that dream, Zolisha was given a mandate straight from heaven to birth, an outreach program geared toward helping women to be more Christ-centered. Thus, Safe Haven Women Outreach was born. Zolisha is the founder and President of the community outreach ministry and currently, the program services the Bloomington-Normal IL Community area. Safe

Haven Women Outreach also has an online presence, and you can find the outreach on Facebook by simply searching the name. Anyone regardless of whether they live in the Bloomington-Normal IL Community or not can follow the page by simply liking the page. During Zolisha's development of the outreach, she continued to pursue her education but at a slower pace while launching the outreach. SHWO's first day of service was April 16, 2016. The program has been said to bring the deliverance power of God and to transform every life that steps within the thresholds of the outreach program. Once the program was fully up and running, Zolisha continued to pursue her education with Liberty University, where she received a Master's degree in Executive Leadership in March of 2017. Zolisha has stated that her education in the secular world has concluded and now has a mandate from Heaven to learn all she can concerning the Kingdom of God. That mandate was met with a call directly from Heaven, telling her to come forth in January 2018. She received the directions from that call in September 2018, informing her in a vision that she would have the authority of Ezekiel to speak to the dry bones of the world and that she would be what Samuel was to Saul and Nathan was to David to many in the body of Christ. Zolisha fully accepted that mandate in January of 2019, where she began to learn the office of the Prophet and has continued to study to show herself approved by the Lord. Since that time, many signs and wonders have followed her by praying for others who have had cyst dried up, minds healed, demons cast out, and miracles such as limbs growing to their proper length. Although many would get excited about the gifts, Zolisha understands that her power does nothing but all by the awesome power of our Lord and Savior Jesus Christ, Zolisha believes that in God, learning never stops, and believes we all should be striving to have the mind of Christ by studying all we can to help us be more like Jesus. Therefore, her studies will continue until the Lord returns.

Contact Info:
Facebook//Instagram: Zolisha L Ware
Website//www.fearlesscenter.com
Facebook//Instagram: Safe Haven Women Outreach
Email: safehavenwomenoutreach@gmail.com

Works Cited

© 2019 Merriam-Webster, I. (2019, May 24). Deceitful. Retrieved from Merriam Webster Dictionary: https://www.merriam-webster.com/dictionary/deceitful

© 2019 Merriam-Webster, I. (2019, May 25). Empowerment. Retrieved from Merriam Webster Dictionary: https://www.merriam-webster.com/dictionary/empowerment

© 2019 Merriam-Webster, I. (2019, May 24). Kind. Retrieved from Merriam Webster Dictionary: https://www.merriam-webster.com/dictionary/kind

© 2019 Merriam-Webster, I. (2019, May 28). Love. Retrieved from Merriam Webster: https://www.merriam-webster.com/dictionary/love

© 2019 Merriam-Webster, I. (2019, May 24). Merriam Webster Dictionary. Retrieved from

Thoughtful: https://www.merriam-webster.com/dictionary/thoughtful

© 2019 Merriam-Webster, I. (2019, May 25). Merriam Webster Dictionary. Retrieved from Harmful: https://www.merriam-webster.com/dictionary/harmful

© 2019 Merriam-Webster, I. (2019, May 25). Satisfying. Retrieved from Merriam Webster Dictionary: https://www.merriam-webster.com/dictionary/satisfying

© 2019 Merriam-Webster, I. (2019, May 24). Spoken. Retrieved from Merriam Webster Dictionary: https://www.merriam-webster.com/dictionary/spoken

2019 Merriam-Webster, I. (2019, May 22). Spoken. Retrieved from Merriam Webster Dictionary: https://www.merriam-webster.com/dictionary/spoken

2020 Merriam-Webster, I. (2020, February 22). Exhortation. Retrieved from Merriam

Webster: https://www.merriam-webster.com/dictionary/exhortation

2020 Merriam-Webster, I. (2020, February 22). Proclamation. Retrieved from Merriam Webster: https://www.merriam-webster.com/dictionary/proclamation

Counter, W. (2020, February 25). How many words are in the bible? Retrieved from Word Counter: https://wordcounter.net/blog/2016/02/21/101241_how-many-pages-are-there-in-the-bible.html

Gateway, B. (2020, February 23). Isaiah 1:3 ESV. Retrieved from Bible Gateway: https://www.biblegateway.com/passage/?search=Isaiah+1%3A3+&version=ESV

Strong LL. D S.T.D, J. (1996). The New Strong's Complete Dictionary of Bible Words. Nashville, Tennessee: Thomas Nelson Publishers.

Strong LLd STD, J. (2010). Strong Exhaustive Concordance of the Bible. Nashville, TN: Thomas Nelson Publishers.

Thompson, F. C. (2007). Thomas and Chain Study Bible. Indianapolis, IN: BB Kirkbride Bible Co. INC.

Webster, M. (2020, February 22). Affirmation. Retrieved from Merriam Webster: https://www.merriam-webster.com/dictionary/affirmation

Index

A

abandonment, 213

affection, 3

anger, 34–36, 238, 246, 286–87

B

battles, 78, 80

bible, 17, 78, 113–14, 168, 236, 246, 256, 292

bitterness, 246, 286

bones, 95

bread, 9, 159, 211, 237

bus, 17

business, 18

C

carnal, 70, 167

cast, 167

child, 18

children, 8, 10, 17–18, 27, 96

Christ, 18, 36, 51, 61, 79–80, 105, 123–24, 140, 157, 271, 275, 285, 289

Comforter, 227

complication, 114

contentment, 77

contradiction, 211

correction, 4, 18, 140

curse, 4, 70, 168, 247, 275

D

death, 19, 112

declarations, 270

decree, 4, 36, 52, 149, 217, 270

deliverance, 211

destiny, 8, 10

discernment, 247

dream, 287

E

edification, 16

education, 286–88

emotions, 17, 237

Empowerment, 112

enemy, 35, 52, 139, 203, 246–47

entitlements, 227

evil, 26, 78

Exclamation, 3

Exhortation, 2

F

faith, 103–5

forgive, 78, 159, 271

forgiveness, 79

forgiving spirit, 184

fruit, 112, 184–85, 274, 278

G

God, 3–5, 8–10, 18, 60, 69–70, 78–79, 104, 139–40, 147–49, 157–59, 166–68, 192–93, 226–29, 254–56, 270–72

gold, 202

grace, 4, 8–9, 11, 16, 26, 123, 139, 141, 184, 274

guard, 2, 11, 25–26, 124, 154, 246

H

HARMFUL WORD, 94

heart, 10–11, 26, 141, 154, 166, 184–85, 194,

203, 237, 246

help, 11, 36, 52, 61, 114, 124, 140–41, 148, 169, 194, 202, 236, 238, 246–47, 255–56

holy nation, 115

husband, 18, 27, 158

I

ignorance, 227–29

J

joy, 70, 183

K

kindness, 11, 59, 237

Kingdom, 255

knowledge, 149

L

leaders, 34, 140

leadership, 140–41

life, 2, 4–6, 18–19, 25–27, 68–70, 78–79, 87, 90, 96, 123–24, 167, 193–94, 237, 255–56, 285

longsuffering, 183

Lord, 11, 33–37, 51–53, 69–71, 79–81, 123–25, 139–41, 149–51, 169, 183–85, 211–13, 237–39, 245–47, 255–57, 285–87

love, 3–4, 30, 36, 105, 112, 123, 139–40, 149, 185, 194, 210–11, 213, 290

M

mercy, 11

mighty, 70, 167

mistreatment, 18, 79

mouth, 4, 6–7, 10, 16, 18–19, 27, 35–36, 95–96, 138, 149, 168, 237–38

multitude, 36, 211

N

negative attributes, 246

net, 60, 113

O

opportuiity, 202

outreach, 288–89

P

pain, 104, 213

pastors, 18, 139

Paul, 70

peace, 78, 95, 154, 183, 202

Power Words, 166

praise, 172

prayer, 11, 19, 27, 36, 52, 61, 70, 96, 104–5, 113–14, 124, 140, 149, 156–59, 185

problem, 10, 114

proclamations, 3

prophet, 139, 289

protection, 203

R

rejection, 213, 238

relationship, 60, 114, 286

responsibility, 18

restorations, 27

righteous, 8, 138

righteousness, 57, 140–41, 227

roots, 5, 105

S

sanctificatioim, 57

scripture, 113

seeds, 246, 254–55

selfish corruption, 78

service, 5, 167

sexual immorality, 287

sins, 27, 36, 105, 138, 211

soul, 7, 59, 77, 105, 166–67, 203, 210, 212

strength, 69–70, 123, 282

strife, 36, 238, 246

strongholds, 70

T

testimonies, 79

tongue, 6, 25, 112, 141, 149

trust, 92, 124, 246

truth, 52, 141, 149, 192–94, 211, 226

U

unrighteousness, 115, 139

V

voice, 52, 224

W

warfare, 70, 140, 167

water, 226, 238, 256

weapons, 70, 203

wisdom, 57, 68, 147–50

world, 3–5, 80, 104, 148, 157, 192, 226

wrath, 34, 36

www.ingramcontent.com/pod-product-compliance
Lightning Source LLC
Chambersburg PA
CBHW071955110526
44592CB00012B/1097